SPECTACULAR RAILROAD PHOTOGRAPHY

A Full Color Guide
to Weather and Lighting Conditions

By Roger M. Ingbretsen

HUNDMAN PUBLISHING
EDMONDS, WASHINGTON

Hundman Publishing
5115 Monticello Drive
Edmonds, Washington 98020

Library of Congress #87-083675

ISBN #0-945434-00-6

Dustjacket Photo by: Roger M. Ingbretsen

Design by: Amie Hundman-Ross
            Cathy Hundman-Lee

Typography by: "DirecType"
                The Type Merchant
                Everett, Washington

Printed in Singapore
by Colour Communications International

4

Roger M. Ingbretsen

Dedicated to my wife and mother, who, like other spouses and parents of "train nuts," have tolerated our lifelong obsession with trains. To Don Ball, Jr., a gentleman.

TABLE OF CONTENTS

Roger M. Ingbretsen

Paul Holtz

INTRODUCTION

The essentials of creative photography are often presented in a highly technical manner and made to sound more complicated than they actually are. One of the reasons for this is that many books deal with the complexities of cameras, lenses and special equipment.

We have approached the subject in a different manner. Because our aim is for you to enjoy railfan photography as you never have before, the techniques presented here are for use with a basic camera. The difference will be in the dramatic results you'll be able to achieve by learning more about how to frame the pictures and focus to use the sun and other available light.

The use of light, time of day, seasons, inclement weather and night photography are all discussed in an effort to help you "see" how to "produce" a creative railroad photograph. It is our hope that these techniques will generate enthusiasm and excitement for the amateur, as well as for the seasoned photographer, and through their simplicity will become part of your technique. If, because of a new-found technique, we can nurture a happy anticipation waiting for that next roll of film to be processed we will share in your pleasure. If the contents of this book help you develop your own personal style, again we revel in your accomplishments. It is through the growth of developing photographers that we will benefit and share the enjoyment of railroading.

Rick Leach

I

The

BASIC

CONCEPT

of Creative

Railfan Photography

The first amber rays of light have just begun stretching their color over the mountains to the east, and the earliest of the early birds are going about doing whatever birds do at the break of dawn. These feathered friends and a cooling cup of coffee are my only companions as my "hunt" nears its exciting climax. A few more moments and the prey will be mine.

The beautiful stillness of the morning is suddenly interrupted by the deep rumblings of diesel engines working in the valley below. It looks as if my plan is going to pay off. My eyes have now focused on the long bridge over Hangman Creek. Fully expecting to see the hard-working engines starting over the bridge at any moment, I'm surprised at how long my wait is extended. I realize now, in the quiet of the morning, how far the sound of the grumbling diesels travels. Finally, after five minutes, the noise of the engines jumps several decibels as the train snakes out from behind the tree line and on to the bridge. It looks as if today's prize will be a quad set of SD40-2's. I ready my weapon — a basic range finder camera — and wait.

The sky has now taken on a warm glow, and the sun is sneaking over the ridge line. I set myself just below roadbed level and make sure my equipment is ready for the shot. The object is to catch the silhouette of the powerful diesels, using the sunrise as my backdrop. From my low angle at trackside, I hope to catch the exhaust in the rays of sunlight and to create a picture of power, movement, and beauty.

As the big green and white units climb the hill and roll into close view, I quickly transform my nostalgic thoughts into the business of fully concentrating on the task at hand — that of taking good railfan photos. Click . . . it's all over for now. In a week, the film will be developed to enjoy and analyze. It will also help organize my next plan of attack.

This may all seem unnecessary and complicated, if not just outright absurd; however, planning, patience, and thinking about what you're trying to accomplish are key ingredients for creative photographs.

Here's a photo (not the one described above) that most photographers would have passed up. With a little more flexibility on your part, shots like this can be yours, too. Remember, your time for roster photography is unchanged.   Roger M. Ingbretsen

Good photography is more than simply buying the most expensive equipment and taking mechanically good pictures. Knowing your subject and how best to work with it add that extra touch.

About a year after I started taking train photos in serious numbers, I realized something was missing in my photographs. As a young boy, I had run around wide-eyed and excited with my Brownie Hawkeye in hand, snapping at anything that rode on rails. That same excitement again took hold when I reached the magic age of forty. I returned to the right-of-way and visited every railroad yard in the area, using roll after roll of Kodak film. I was very content taking pictures of every engine and caboose that came within focus of my ever-present camera lens. When you take a lot of pictures, you're bound to get some interesting ones — which I did — but for the most part, the vast majority of my photos were not very exciting.

To correct this situation, I started digesting book after book and magazine upon magazine. The reason for my research was to discover which pictures gave me that feeling of wanting to be there.

Certain things stood out about many of the better-than-average photos. They were taken at sunrise, sunset, in rain, fog, or some other element of nature. Additionally, headlights, signal lights, or exhaust were often present to give the picture action or a sense of movement. These items then became the benchmark I used, whenever possible, to add creativity to my railroad photography. Of course, to capture these elements in my photos, I would have to be in the right place, at the right time, and under the right conditions. I was about to become what I call a "foul weather photographer."

As in most successful ventures, a plan aids in learning or remembering a technique. In this case, we'll divide the subject into three major areas. They are: equipment, subject, and conditions.

On the first leg of our journey, let's cover the use of your equipment or camera. The following six points or pre-

The most difficult part of shooting in the fog is the willingness to drop what you're doing when the condition occurs. Get a friend interested enough to join you and you're more likely to get this kind of shot.

Roger M. Ingbretsen

cautions will enhance your chances of taking good photos.

*Be extremely careful when loading your camera. Make sure the film is advanced all the way to "1" on the exposure counter. I learned this the hard way when only half a picture developed of an excellent snow scene. Each time you load film, make sure the film speed, "ASA" number, is set properly for the speed film you're using.

*Keep your camera on the same setting at all times when not in use. This way, when you grab your camera for those unexpected shots, you'll have a starting point to work from. Most rail photos are taken at infinity and higher number (smaller aperture) f-stop settings. My camera is always set at f16, infinity, and 250 speed. Keep extra film with you at all times. Some days you just can't miss getting that perfect picture. Not having film is one of the most frustrating situations in which a photographer can find himself, especially when conditions are perfect.

*While on the subject of film, I highly recommend the use of Kodak Kodachrome 64 film when taking 35mm transparencies. Because of it's consistent quality, it is preferred by most photographers I know. Kodachrome and Fuji film are preferred for printing reproduction. This film also has some very forgiving qualities when taking photos under less-than-optimum light conditions. In my larger format camera, I use Ektachrome 64 or 100 professional film and have it processed by Kodak for the best consistent results. Kodachrome has just become available in 120 size.

*Concentrate on holding your camera very steady. I found myself so mesmerized by the sound of the five-chime whistle while shooting an approaching Amtrak, the photograph became secondary and a good action shot was missed. For low speed settings, try to brace your camera against something. At low numbered settings, your movement will result in a blurred picture.

*Take several shots of the same scene at

The best snow shots are made just after the snow has fallen, especially if you're in an industrial area where snow quickly becomes dirty and dusty.

Roger M. Ingbretsen

different f-stop settings above and below what your light meter indicates as correct. Different exposures can create entirely different moods. Chances are you'll never be at the same place under the same conditions, so take those extra pictures to make sure you get what you came after. Film is cheap in comparison to the cost of getting there.

*Make a few basic notes during your photo excursions. This can include camera setting, angle of shot, lighting, time of day, or weather conditions. These notes will be helpful in determining your camera's capabilities, as well as your ability to use it. Specifically, you'll learn what combinations work best for you.

Now that we have covered equipment precautions, let's discuss the subject . . . trains. Knowing where, when, and how often your subject is going to be available is a must. Just like a hunter, if you're not looking or waiting in the right place, your prey (a train) will not be shot. Here are five ways to increase your chances of having a successful hunt.

*Talk to other railfans, historians, or modelers, and if you can locate a railroad photographer, all the better. It never ceases to amaze me how friendly and open people are who share our enthusiasm for railroading. Very often, the local railfan can give you information not available anywhere else, including the folks who work the railroads.

*Talk to trainmen or anyone connected with the railroad. Engineers, conductors, brakemen, repair men, and track maintenance crews can fill you in on the area's activity.

*If there is a yard or switch tower nearby, establish a rapport with the dispatcher or tower operator. They can provide a wealth of information on train movements, as well as relay ideas on locations to catch a train in the right setting.

*Timetables of Amtrak will help you find the elusive passenger train for your lens to capture. Most freight trains also run on schedules. Odd-numbered trains run west, and even-numbered trains run east.

One technique in fog or haze is to keep an object close so that its detail highlights the lack of detai on distant objects.

Jay Williams

*Stake out your territory. Bridges, tunnels, high vantage points, yards, crossings, interesting topography, signal lights, and semaphore locations all add to a picture. Discover back roads to interesting locations. "Sight your lens" to see if it may be worth coming back to at a later date or at a different time of day. What looks ordinary in bright sunlight may be just right for a sunset picture.

To round out our excursion into the world of "creative railfan photography," let's discuss the third and final leg of our formula . . . photographic conditions. My advice at this point is to "get an image" in your head, think about it, and then try to create it. As a rule, I now find myself in the worst weather conditions, hence the term "foul weather photographer." Additionally, getting up very early to capture the first rays of sunlight, or hanging around in the late afternoon for that special sunset, has caused me on occasion to rearrange my sleeping and eating habits. This is a complete switch from how I took photos a short two years ago. Then, it was bright, sunny days between 11 a.m. and 2 p.m.

Foul weather photography does have its inconvenient moments, but it's fun, a change of pace, and will deliver some spectacular results. One word to the wise. Take every precaution to keep your photographic equipment as dry as possible. Keeping your camera in a protective case or bag when not in use and having an umbrella handy when shooting are two ways to cope with the problem. I wear a baseball cap. The visor helps keep rain and snow off the camera when shooting. I also protect the camera from the elements by carrying it under my jacket. Now, on with the elements!

*Rain . . . rain is the most diverse of all weather conditions to photograph. A stormy sky, just after a cloudburst and with shafts of sunlight streaming through, will give a dramatic effect to any rail scene. In the rain, bright objects such as a signal light or headlight show up clearly and add punch to a picture. In fact, any bright color will provide impact. Rain will also provide

Night photography is a field all its own. In general, the most effective shots can be taken with incidental light (the natural lighting around the subject). Flash can be used, but that's not the subject of this book.

Roger M. Ingbretsen

a fresh-washed look to rail equipment – a condition not usually associated with trains. Finally, rain produces great reflectivity for an excellent effect. After a rain, the standing water in a yard or alongside the right-of-way has great reflecting quality and can provide some interesting possibilities.

*Fog . . . this element is the hardest to capture unless you live in London. It's not a predictable season or weather condition. Finding this dense condition to shroud your subject is the hard part, but the mystique that surrounds a train slicing through the fog is a picture worth every ounce of effort you can muster.

*Snow . . . just after or during a snowfall you will find excellent possibilities. Because nothing has disturbed the landscape, the first run-through of a train as it plows and swirls up the fresh powdery white stuff is an exciting event to capture. It's definitely an action shot worth going after. Late afternoon and early morning photos taken during a snowfall will create an eerie, cold effect. Again, as in rain, pictures taken on a gray day with snow on the ground, provide a great background for bright, colorful objects. If you want to portray a feeling of cold, I mean icy cold, take a picture of the tail end of a caboose after it has completed a journey through a slightly wet snow storm. The snow and ice collect on the back ladders, steps, and railings because of the air-flow over and around the back of the train. A low angle shot when frost, snow, or ice is on the cross ties or on a switch machine, with the rail equipment in the background, lends a certain crispness to your winter scenes.

*Sunrise – Sunset . . . these "golden hours" of early morning and late afternoon produce a warm amber to reddish tinge, having a dramatic effect on your subject. Shadows can range in any degree from black to soft muted tan or gray. The sun at its low angle placed behind your subject will take advantage of backlighting and create a great silhouette image. Shooting indirectly into the sun when it's at a low angle can produce a photo containing great

All of the photos in this book were taken with a normal lens, without flash and without special filters, just simply enough enthusiasm to get out when the weather conditions created great opportunities.

Roger M. Ingbretsen

rivet and louver detail on the side of an engine. Many of us have been taught to put the sun either behind us or over our shoulder when taking photos. Forget that myth. Try shooting into the sun. I shoot many pictures from out of the shadows. Keep the sun just off to the left or right of the lens. Use your hand, a pole, a tree, or piece of rolling stock to shadow your lens from direct sunlight if possible. This technique will open a whole new area of photographic possibilities.

Countless authors have used "bright, gleaming ribbons of rail" or some variation of these words to describe a railroad scene. Low angle pictures taken at sunrise or sunset and looking down a rail line produce a vivid testimonial to these words. Don't forget the obvious — your favorite rail equipment with a beautiful sunrise or sunset sky as the backdrop. A brilliant sky can make even the most insensitive person stop and look, if just for a moment, and wonder about creation itself.

Where you live definitely has a great influence on the photos you take. Snow scenes in Florida are quite unlikely, but beautiful sunsets and rain squalls are very possible. Every location — whether north, south, east, or west — mountains, hills, flatland, or desert — has a natural beauty or element all its own which, if used advantageously, can lend a whole new dimension to your photography. Experiment with your environment. Try the unusual and be creative.

Two additional points: First, be safe when around railroad equipment. Because of its very nature, injuries are certainly possible where railroad equipment is concerned. Go slow and watch what you're doing. Second, be friendly. Being friendly is what railroad people are all about.

It takes a lot of looking and a certain amount of luck to find that creative photograph. But when all the elements of the formula fit together — the equipment, subject, and condition — you'll feel a great sense of accomplishment! You'll have taken the perfect railfan photo!

For sunrise or sunset shots, silhouetting structures or railway equipment can be most effective. Use part of the structure to block out the sun. Here, it's the leg of the bridge closest to the rail that gets between the lens and the sun just peaking over the horizon.

Roger M. Ingbretsen

2

The Splendor of a
SUNRISE

There is something very vibrant and yet relaxing about a sunrise. Movement is beginning, but the quiescence of the night is still present. Like the setting in motion of 8,000 horsepower at the head of a freight car consist, the world begins to move slowly, deliberately, and dramatically. The photographer's goal is to capture this crescendo of power and beauty on film.

The most difficult aspect of sunrise railroad photography is simply getting out of bed to travel to that special location. The color and beauty are available. All one has to do is be at the right place early enough.

No two sunrise skies are the same. Each has its own distinct color or tone. Add a few clouds and the variations are endless. Also, because of the tilt of the earth's axis, the sun rises in a slightly different location each day. This results in a changing effect of shadow and side or backlighting on a daily basis. Over a period of months, this change is dramatic. An object previously sidelighted by the sun's early rays could later be silhouetted against the rising sun.

Predicting the exact point on the horizon where the sun will first appear can be difficult. The sun will rise to the north of east during the summer in the United States and southern Canada, but in the winter, it will rise to the south of east. You may want to take an initial field trip to determine where the sun will rise in relation to where you plan on taking your pictures. You can then arrange your subject to take advantage of the rising sun. A compass can be a worthwhile tool as well.

Sunrise is very easy to photograph because exposure is not critical. If you open up your lens too wide, the scene will simply look brighter, as if it were taken later in the day. If you close your lens (higher f-stop), the scene will appear darker and less detailed. The key is to bracket your exposure. Take one shot at the automatic exposure or suggested meter reading; make additional shots, one or two stops, with less exposure; and make several shots, one or two stops, with more exposure. After the pictures are developed, you can choose which scene best portrays the mood you're trying to convey.

When discussing a sunrise, an analysis of the impact of light is a must. Photography is a "looking" experience; therefore, light is a crucial element in the formulation of a picture. The light in a picture communicates through our eyes a message and emotion just as the words and sounds of a song communicate a message and emotion through our ears. If, as a photographer, you learn to use natural light to communicate a message, mood, or emotion — no matter what your personal style or technique — you will have mastered the essence of photography.

The exploitation of light defines shapes, outlines the subject, and conveys texture, depth, and contrast. Keeping these points in mind, it's easy to see the importance of light and its effect on creating that perfect railfan picture. Because of the ease with which sunrise sunlight can be photographed, sunrise scenes are an excellent starting point for experimenting.

PRECEDING PAGE LARGE: Ironically, we start off the sunrise chapter with a sunset picture. This has been done purposely to stress a point. In many situations, it's virtually impossible to tell in a photo the difference between the two. Also, much of what is explained in this chapter applies to sunsets just as much of what is explained in the sunset chapter applies to capturing a beautiful sunrise. Some of the most striking sunrise/sunset pictures occur when the sun is below the horizon as demonstrated by this photo.
Ektachrome 64, 1/60 sec, f5.6
Roger M. Ingbretsen

PRECEDING PAGE SMALL: Almost total black in the foreground and the main subject of the engine contrast sharply with the color of the sky. This picture has impact because of its bold contrast and very specific form. Walk around your subject and look for this effect.
Ektachrome 64, 1/50 sec, f4.5
Roger M. Ingbretsen

RIGHT: The sky is a mixture of orange, gray, and golden yellow at the horizon. A combination of these colors is picked up on the side of the diesel equipment.
Ektachrome 64, 1/60 sec, f5.6
Roger M. Ingbretsen

FOLLOWING PAGE: These two pictures were taken at the same location on two successive days. Adding texture to an ordinary string of box cars was accomplished with extreme side angle lighting from the rising sun. Convergence adds to the photo. Note how the box cars, rails and telephone poles all lead to the overpass located almost dead center in the pictures. In the inset picture, the appearance of early morning fog at the left was created by driving my car along a dry, dusty access road. Starting from the bridge, I drove to where my camera was set up, stopped and ran quickly to the camera and took the picture. The camera was set with identical f-stop and speed of 5.6 and 125 on both occasions. The "dusty" fog was used to shield the direct rays of the sun just above the horizon from the camera lens.
Ektachrome 64
Roger M. Ingbretsen

TOP: The strong colors of a rising sun can blot out the actual color of an object. Here the metal side of a green engine takes on the yellow-orange color tones of early sun. This splash of vibrant color adds impact to an otherwise ordinary picture.
Kodachrome 64, 1/125 sec, f5.6

ABOVE: A stunning pre-sunrise sky, rich with multi-colored clouds has a dramatic effect on the silhouetted railroad equipment in the lower half of the scene. A brilliant sky can make even the most insensitive person stop and look, if just for a moment.
Kodachrome 64, 1/60 sec, f5.6

FACING PAGE: The early morning quiet is broken by the grumbling of the approaching diesels. Like the setting in motion of 8,000 horsepower at the head end of a freight train, the world begins to move in the early morning hours.

All Photos by Roger M. Ingbretsen

This was a "planned" early morning silhouette shot. The position had been staked out the previous day, so the approximate location of the sun rising above the horizon would be known. Getting in close at the roadbed level would put the sun behind the engines from sunrise to a five degree sun elevation. This would allow 30 minutes for a scheduled freight to be captured in a side angle silhouette shot; however, as the picture unfolded within the viewfinder, the sun, just cresting the horizon ahead of the approaching train, provided a shot with more impact. Note how the exhaust is made more apparent by the side lighting of the sun. Also, the cold morning has added a touch of frost to objects in the foreground.   Ektachrome 64, 1/250 sec, f5.6

Roger M. Ingbretsen

ABOVE: Some of the wildest color variations can be captured during the few minutes when the first rays of the sun are caught as they light up the underside of a cloud formation. Here the bright colors accent the black silhouette of a railroad bridge photographed during a long train wait which never materialized.
Kodachrome 64, 1/125 sec, f5.6

ABOVE: The contrast of dark foreground highlights the bright silvered rails as they reflect the early morning light. Depth is created as the rails converge on the eastern horizon and meet the rising sun in the top third of the picture. This is a classic example of symmetry.   Kodachrome 64, 1/60 sec, f5.6

FOLLOWING PAGE: The exploitation of light helps define shapes, outlines the subject, conveys texture, depth, and contrast. Keeping all these points in mind, it is easy to see the importance of light and its effect on creating that perfect railfan picture.
Ektachrome 100, 1/60 sec, f5.6

All Photos by Roger M. Ingbretsen

3

The Mystique of
FOG

Fog produces a quality suggestive of adventure. Because it tends to envelop distant objects and drain the overall scene of color, additional interest is given to the main subject. A train seems to actually penetrate, or rather come out of, the weather. A low angle view emphasizing the foreground tracks helps create an even greater impression of distance in a scene. This is because the pale, almost fragile light produces a scene darker in the foreground and lighter in the distance. This, coupled with an oncoming engine's headlight searching for the next milepost, creates a picture for the viewer to linger over.

Successful photography in the poor light of fog or failing light does not require special cameras or lenses. Rather, it is a matter of experience and patience. One word of caution. Be careful not to overexpose a picture taken in mist or fog. In fact, underexpose by one-half to two stops for the best results. In fog, millions of tiny water molecules are suspended in air. This diffuses the light and creates a muted and subtle scene. The strong, emphatic shape of an engine stands out well against the blue-gray or milky-white background produced by fog; however, distant shapes melt or merge into this milky-white haze. The headlight of a train piercing through fog appears more red-orange than usual, because the light vapor disperses the blue color spectrum, yet allows the rays of red to penetrate more directly. Film is much more sensitive to the ultraviolet components of haze, mist, or fog than the human eye. This means pictures will automatically exaggerate the effects of these elements. This magic element provides an even deeper penetrating "mood" in pictures than in real life.

Most low light photographs – sunrise, sunset, rain, or fog – create a specific mood for the viewer. Fog creates one of the strongest natural moods in photography.

Understanding where and how fog forms can aid you in your search for pictures. Overland fog usually forms just after sunset. An evening fog begins when the sky is clear. As the sun goes down, the earth radiates heat into the clear sky and the air above the ground becomes cool. As the temperature drops below the dew point, fog is formed. Heat from the sun the next morning, aided by slight morning winds, usually dissipates the fog. This is called radiation fog.

Advection fog is formed when warm air passes over cold land or a cold body of water. The same is true when cold air passes over warm land or warm water. The first warm days of spring coupled with the still very cold runoff waters of winter are a good mix for producing fog. The first real cold snap in the fall mixed with the warm waters of summer also provide the proper conditions for fog to form.

Fog tends to simplify shapes, enhance the sense of distance, and reduce color or tonal values. It's easy to see how the romance and nostalgia of railroading can be greatly enhanced when using fog as an ingredient.

PRECEDING PAGE LARGE: A "hot-shot" freight train bolts out of the fog at fifty plus miles per hour. The strong, emphatic shape of the oncoming train is distinctive, identifiable, and stands out against the milky-white background. A photo like this can accept some blur if the light isn't strong enough.
Ektachrome 64, 1/250 sec, f4.5
Roger M. Ingbretsen

PRECEDING PAGE SMALL: Casting a defused light, the sun comes through the fog as a soft, yellow ball. Taking pictures directly into the sun can be easily accomplished when using the natural element of fog as a filter. In fact, this method may add significantly to the photo.
Kodachrome 64, 1/125 sec, f5.6
Roger M. Ingbretsen

RIGHT: A late afternoon winter fog casts a shroud over the entire scene as this train picks its way through the "soup". The combination of the warm air and cold snow is what produced the fog for this picture. Understanding where and how fog forms can aid in your search for the right conditions.
Ektachrome 64, 1/125 sec, f5.6
Roger M. Ingbretsen

LEFT: Almost all color has been drained from this scene, resulting in an extreme black-to-white picture. Distant shapes have literally melted into the background. Observe-Observe-Observe! You'll see plenty of photo opportunities where none seemed to exist before. Kodachrome 64, 1/125sec, f5.6

TOP: A long wait on a cold, foggy day in the fall did not result in a train shot. Instead, I ended up with a striking picture of the sun rising through the fog, surrounding the bridge in shafts of sunlight. It was worth the wait. This "straight-into-the-sun" shot is proof that "breaking the rules" in photography can produce stunning results.
Kodachrome, 1/60 sec, f5.6

ABOVE: Mist rising off a glass-like river surface imparts a gauze-like veil. The small clump of weeds in the foreground and the trees behind the bridge supply the scene with front-to-back distance. The bridge appears to be suspended over the river with the supports having no visible entry into the water.
Kodachrome 64, 1/125sec, f4.5

All Photos by Roger M. Ingbretsen

TOP LEFT: Where has our diesel friend been and where is he going? The massive bulk of the oncoming engine, with its headlight searching for the next milepost, creates a striking picture.
Kodachrome 64, 1/125 sec, f4.5

TOP RIGHT: The sun appears as a yellow disk as it shines through the early morning haze. Telephone wires, the SD40-2's with tanker tenders, and the darkened roadbed are all silhouetted against the lighter skyline in the distance.
Kodachrome 64, 1/250 sec, f4.5

ABOVE LEFT: It's a dreary, dismal, and rainy day at the railroad yards. The fog has reduced tonal values and allowed the blue-gray colors to take over. Distant dots of light bleeding through the fog are the only indication of life in the area.
Kodachrome 64, 1/60 sec, f4.5

ABOVE RIGHT: With a burst of exhaust, the hard working diesel slowly rumbles off into the mysterious unknown. Catching exhaust on film is one of those details which adds action or motion to your railroad photography — even in the fog.
Kodachrome 64, 1/125 sec, f4.5

FACING PAGE: An oncoming train is caught on film just as it is about to break out of a fog bank. The sun had just begun to burn off the early morning fog. This "burn-off" can happen quickly, as was the case on this very cold morning.
Ektachrome 64, 1/250 sec, f5.6

All Photos by Roger M. Ingbretsen

ABOVE: A light fog superbly accentuates the foreground
in this picture. The jewelled headlights add that necessary
spark to catch the eye of the viewer.
Norfolk & Western Photograph

TOP: A "distinctive beam" of light penetrates the blue color spectrum as this switch engine slowly emerges from a dense evening fog. Film is much more sensitive to the ultraviolet components of haze, mist, or fog than is the human eye. This means that pictures exaggerate these elements and produce a more definite beam of light in a photo than can be seen with the human eye.   Kodachrome 64, 1/60 sec, f5.6
Roger M. Ingbretsen

ABOVE: Snow on the ground and fog in the air are not an unusual combination. They can be combined to give an almost eerie veil to a night scene.
Kodachrome 64, 5 sec, f4.5
Fred M. Simon

4

The Versatility of
RAIN

Because rain seems unfriendly to the art of photography, most photographers put their cameras away during this adverse weather condition. Rain and its effect on railroad equipment, however, can produce some very dazzling results.

Poor lighting conditions are normally what you deal with during inclement weather situations. Color values tend to darken and blend together; however, clarity and detail can, in some instances, actually be enhanced by the lack of light. Many details, which are hidden by the shadows produced in bright sun, can be seen more clearly in the subdued light of rain or overcast skies. This is especially true with the underframes of cars and engines.

Rainfall also gives a glassy, gleaming appearance to hard surfaces such as those found around railroads and associated facilities. Like a fresh coat of varnish on a beautiful oak floor, the wetness of rain enhances the sometimes drab colors of rail equipment. Additionally, bright objects such as lights or polished metal stand out spectacularly in the normally dim low light of a rainy overcast sky. Look for these touches of bright color on a rainy day. They'll add that extra spark and punctuate the picture with interest.

Definitely take pictures immediately after a rain shower. Surfaces will still be wet and shiny, and most of the time, the light will be brighter. Also, puddles found in rail yards or ditches along the right-of-way will reflect beautifully the sky, the subject, and its surroundings.

Play with alignment of reflections. Camera placement, looking through and moving your lens, and framing the scene can all be keys to capturing on film a truly interesting photo. Experiment with different exposures as well. Underexposing a full one to two stops will allow the highlighted areas in the picture to become a bit more isolated from the shadowy areas. Add a sunrise or sunset sky to your reflective railroad scene, and you can't miss creating a picture you'll be proud of.

Don't forget that cloud formations can also be very dramatic just after a passing shower. Compose beautiful clouds with a reflective water surface and rail equip-

ment, and you'll provide that extra bonus toward creating a truly great photo.

If getting your camera wet disturbs you, don't forget to use the protection of overhangs, canopies, or even your car to take photographs in the rain. This technique can help keep you and your equipment out of the elements. Remember, if you're willing to brave the elements and become a "foul weather photographer," you'll be amply rewarded.

PRECEDING PAGE LARGE: A long freight pulls out onto the mainline during a rain-soaked October day. This picture was shot from the dry comfort of my car. The point: When possible, use whatever shelter is available to keep both you and your equipment dry during foul weather photography trips.
Ektachrome 100, 1/125 sec, f5.6
Roger M. Ingbretsen

PRECEDING PAGE SMALL: Most photographers put their cameras away during adverse weather conditions, because rain seems unfriendly to the art of photography. Nothing could be further from the truth. Rain and its effect on railroad equipment can produce some very interesting results.
Ektachrome 400 film-800
Robert Huron

RIGHT: These two shots were taken with the camera actually sitting on top of the rail. With an f-stop of 32, clear depth of field is obtained from within inches of the camera out to infinity. Note how the engines' headlights are reflected differently on the dry and wet rail. Use the smallest lense opening (largest number f-stop) that motion in the photo will allow.
Ektachrome 64, 1/30 sec
Roger M. Ingbretsen

ABOVE: Here the red signal lights pierce the overcast sky and reflect on the wet roadway. Only in foul weather conditions could you create such an original photograph.

Kodachrome 64, 1/125 sec, f5.6

RIGHT: Two red block signal lights stab into a dismal evening sky while an approaching train swings off the mainline at a fairly high speed. This speed, combined with low light conditions, tends to blur the train's lights, and creates a sense of action. Ektachrome 64, 1/125 sec, f4.5

FOLLOWING PAGE TOP: A damp, dull day is invaded by this branchline freight as it rumbles slowly by. The engine lights, which accent the darkest area of the picture, provide a beginning focal point. The mud and debris on the trackwork is typical of a "once-a-day" branchline operation.

Kodachrome 64, 1/125 sec, f5.6

FOLLOWING PAGE LOWER LEFT: The falling rain has blurred the mirror image of the engine in the standing pool of water. The circles of rippling water caused by the raindrops help give a wet, damp feeling to the scene.

Ektachrome 100, 1/250 sec, f5.6

FOLLOWING PAGE LOWER RIGHT: Reflections and artificial light can be the key to turning a simple rainy day photograph into one of drama. Don't pass up this kind of opportunity. All Photos by Roger M. Ingbretsen

TOP LEFT: A passing rain storm combines with a setting sun to wash this freight train in a warm, golden glow. A red switch light adds punch and balance to this photograph. Don't pass up a scene like this just because there is no engine or caboose. The flavor is still very much "railroad."   Kodachrome 64, 1/125 sec, f8

LEFT: Don't just aim and shoot at your main subject. Instead, look through the view finder and move around to create the best possible picture. In this photo, combining the reflective qualities of water on the rails and low light conditions produces an eye-catching photo.   Kodachrome 64, 1/125 sec, f5.6

ABOVE: Another reflective water scene is used to point out the versatility of this type of photography. In this picture, the focus of attention is the standing water itself; and the train plays a secondary role to the slightly masked sun and its reflection in the water.   Ektachrome 64, 1/125 sec, f8

All Photos by Roger M. Ingbretsen

ABOVE: Only the rainy-day photographer could shoot the special effects of a rain-soaked platform. The lights tend to jump out at the viewer.
Kodachrome 64, 1/125 sec, f4.5
Bruce Nall

RIGHT: A stormy day, a train, and a camera mix well. Rain can be the most versatile of all weather conditions in which to photograph. Here the storm clouds hang low over the mountains, the dirt road at the left glistens with wetness, and the lights highlight the front of these rain-washed blue and white SD60 engines.
Ektachrome 100, 1/125 sec, f5.6
Roger M. Ingbretsen

5

The Cover of
SNOW

The toughness, stability, and dependability of railroading come through loud and clear when railroads are photographed in cold, snowy conditions. It's as if to say, "We get through no matter what the weather." This same determination applies to the photographer who braves the cold elements to capture on film the "magic of railroading in the snow."

Some very special problems are encountered when taking pictures in the cold weather associated with snow. Cold can weaken batteries, thicken the lubricant in your camera, and make film brittle. Additionally, because of the dry air associated with cold weather, the presence of electrostatic discharge (ESD) can cause sparking on your film, marking the image. Advance and rewind film slowly; take extra batteries; and try to keep your camera warm, but not hot. If travelling in your car to a photo location, avoid storing your camera next to a heating vent. When you step outside to take a picture, your entire camera can fog up or even ice over.

One precaution not thought of often is the prevention of "fog over" of your lens from your breath. If you have a habit of blowing on the lens to clean it off — don't! Your warm breath in cold weather will fog over the lens and render the camera useless when it's time to take a picture. Instead, position yourself to take the picture, hold your breath, bring the camera up to shooting position, snap, bring the camera away from your face, and breathe. Although it sounds complicated, it's a necessary precaution for very cold weather. Also, when going inside after shooting in cold weather, don't let your camera warm up too fast. Condensation can form inside the lens or on the film.

Snow and ice scenes tend to underexpose. This is because your light meter will read high due to the great reflectivity of the bright, white snow mixed with sunlight. One way to avoid this is to take an exposure reading off the palm of your hand or a medium gray surface. If you're using an automatic camera reading, chances are you'll have to disregard its instruction. As is stated several times throughout this book, bracket your shot a

stop or two in both directions to be sure you get what you need. Remember, film is cheap in comparison to the cost of getting you there.

The cover of snow hides much of the surroundings in a white blanket. Thus, a specific piece of railroad equipment can become very central to a picture's composition. Snow scenes can create some exceptional opportunities for crisp color contrast. A blue sky will cause the shadowy areas of a snow scene to assume a blue cast. This, however, can help emphasize the very coldness you're trying to portray in a winter photo. Under an overcast sky, snow takes on a more gray or leaden appearance, leaning toward a blue cast. As in fog, this overall grayness can provide an excellent background for the vivid colors in signal lights or brightly painted railroad equipment. Making use of this highlighting of color can create a focus on certain parts of your photo and develop interest.

When it is actually snowing, pictures will look about the same as when taken in the milky-white gauziness of fog. Again, as in fog, engines stand out well in a snow storm because of the bulkiness and boldness of their massive shapes. Photographed at the correct exposure, snowflakes can be seen in the beam of the engine's headlight. Streaks or flakes of snow can be best photographed using a slow shutter speed and sidelighting against a dark background. Don't use a flash when it's snowing. The bright light will bounce back off the closest flakes and show virtually nothing of the scene you're photographing.

A fresh, new-fallen snow — when branches are heavy and white — can create a very picturesque railroad scene. To add more beauty to your snow shot, take your photos in early morning or late evening light. Snow crystals will glisten, and more form and texture will be added to the white ground cover. Also, because of its great reflectivity, the snow can aid in making hand-held pictures when little light is available from the sky.

Putting aside all the technical and physical precautions you must consider while photographing in cold weather, railroad pictures can take on a whole new look and form when shot during this inclement situation. You'll enjoy a sense of accomplishment when viewing your handiwork from the warmth of your home.

PRECEDING PAGE LARGE: On a cold afternoon in February, in the Canadian Rockies' Kicking Horse Pass, this trio of hard working diesels growl toward the summit. You'll enjoy a real sense of accomplishment when viewing your handiwork from the warmth of your home.
Ektachrome 100, 1/250 sec, f5.6
Roger M. Ingbretsen

PRECEDING PAGE SMALL: A cold, moonlit sky casts a blue glow on the snow-covered ground while a distant fog melts the background and horizon into one. The trackwork in the foreground and the headlight of an oncoming train furnish the two key points for a well composed winter night scene.
Kodachrome 64, 1 sec, f4.5
Roger M. Ingbretsen

UPPER RIGHT: A very cold, crisp morning catches a hot freight "singing" along the cold ribbons of steel. Snow scenes can create some exceptional opportunities for crisp color contrast.
Ektachrome, 1/250 sec, f8
Roger M. Ingbretsen

LOWER RIGHT: A new-fallen snow — when branches are heavy and white — can create a very picturesque railroad scene. Shot at high noon from the shadows, the white branches of these pine trees have taken on distinctive form.
Ektachrome 64, 1/250 sec, f11
Roger M. Ingbretsen

LEFT: A late evening photo takes on a cold, bleak appearance under the right lighting conditions. Most of the detail is gone and a feeling or mood is captured rather that just a picture.
Ektachrome 64, 1/125 sec, f5.6
Roger M. Ingbretsen

ABOVE: You can almost feel the snow crunch under your feet in this winter scene. Low sunlight has added excellent texture and depth to this photograph.
Rick Leach

FOLLOWING PAGES: With the use of dark shadows across the nose of these approaching diesels, the headlights appear bright even in sunlight. The long shadows common during northern winters can help in creating bold contrast in your photos. Use them!
Ektachrome 100, 1/250 sec, f8
Roger M. Ingbretsen

ABOVE LEFT AND TOP RIGHT: These two Union Pacific engine photos demonstrate what walking around the subject and looking through your lens can do to change the overall compsition of a picture. When the subject looks interesting, take a lot of pictures from many different angles. Kodachrome 64, 1/125 sec, f5.6

ABOVE RIGHT: Just in from a run, the caboose of this train shows the combined effects of a wet snowstorm and a moving train. The result is cold and chilling.

Kodachrome 64, 1/125 sec, f5.6

FACING PAGE: The "Canadian" offers its passengers the majesty of the untamed west as no other train in North America. Passing a westbound freight, the eastbound passenger train of fluted stainless steel sweeps around a curve clicking off the nostalgic miles. Developing a good feeling and interesting picture in all seasons, through good basic photography techniques, is a goal worth shooting for. Watch for good color contrast. Here the yellow sulfur adds dramatically to the photo. Ektachrome 100, 1/250 sec, f8

All Photos by Roger M. Ingbretsen

INSET PHOTOS: These standard "Three-Quarter" shots demonstrate the different pictures which can be made under three types of snow conditions. First, a train kicks up powder on a cold March day. Second, snowflakes become visible against the dark color of the train. Third, long and cold shadows cast a special feeling of bitter cold across this January snow scene.

Kodachrome
Tim Lund

BELOW: A light, wet snow has covered the ballast just enough to develop an interesting ground cover. The lights and exhaust of the train provide a sense of motion, and the red and green signal light are a definite eye catcher.

Kodachrome
Roger M. Ingbretsen

6

The Serenity of a

SUNSET

As old as the scene may seem, the classic "ride off into the sunset" remains a proven success formula. Few photographers can resist making a picture of a sunset. Additionally, few individuals can resist pausing just a bit longer to look at an exceptional sunset photo. Throw in the ribbons of silver or the powerful silhouette of railroad equipment and it's hard to miss creating that special sought-after mood.

The scattering of light rays by air, dust, and water vapour all contribute to the beautiful yellow, orange, and red colors we witness at sunset. Because the sun must penetrate more atmosphere at a very low angle during this period, the blue wave lengths are scattered more easily, thus allowing the other hues of the color spectrum to dominate. In many cases, it's hard to tell the difference between a sunrise or sunset picture, because they're intrinsically the same.

There are some conditions; however, that contribute to major differences between the two. The sky is usually clean in the morning, but stagnant air or early morning mist can greatly alter the appearance of the sun. One of our modern contributions – pollution – creates hazy red or orange sunsets. This is why sunsets are often more spectacular than sunrises.

Because color changes occur very quickly during a sunset, take plenty of pictures as the color unfolds before your eyes. Don't wait for what you feel may be the best color photo, or the rapid changes might rob you of a great shot before you realize it. Remember, sunsets develop, change, and then disappear very quickly due to certain cloud cover conditions. Once again, bracket your pictures a stop or two above and below normal f-stop settings.

As is true for sunrise photos, some of the most striking sunset pictures occur when the sun is below the horizon. If weather conditions are right – cloud cover overhead, but no clouds beyond or at the horizon – the sun's rays will color the underside of the clouds. This condition, coupled with an average amount of pollution, can add up to some very wild colors. When shooting sunset pictures under these conditions, use a tripod or brace yourself to keep your camera as stationary as possible. Your shutter speed will be slow and any movement could ruin a fantastic photo.

Additional exposures are a must if you include the disk of sun in your picture. The brightness of the sun, even at the low light level of sunset, will elevate the meter reading, so a picture may come out underexposed and darker than expected. Add one or two stops of exposure to counteract this problem. Also, taking a picture with the sun shining in your lens can create sun glare spots in your photo. These spots can, in some instances, actually add to the scene. Don't shy away from taking pictures into the sun. Take the chance. The rewards are worth it.

Silhouettes are one of the most effective uses of sunset or sunrise photography. Because interest is drawn to the subject as well as to the beautiful sky, an exciting scene will be created. Exploit the different shooting angles and take full advantage of the fantastic backlighting produced by these low angle, low light conditions. A warm, golden glow or pink-to-red color – with the massive, almost black silhouette of an engine in the foreground – smacks of boldness and beauty.

The lure of faraway places, travel, railroads, and all they encompass can be given added meaning and form by using this element of nature. The sunset does indeed hold universal appeal.

PRECEDING PAGE LARGE: A very low sun here just at sunset gives the reflection off of not only the rails, but the crossing gate structure and the wooden deck of the crossing itself. The highlights and dramatic effect are worth striving for. Opportunities like this occur almost every day, yet most of us with camera in hand bypass them.

PRECEDING PAGE SMALL: When shooting from a kneeling position, the steel rails produce an exaggerated perspective as they converge toward the horizon. The setting sun creates a halo of yellow and pink on the underside of the clouds.
Kodachrome 64, 1/60 sec, f4.5

UPPER RIGHT: The bold lines of the engine are emphasized by this low angle "look-up" shot. The setting sun helps light up the face of the engine and provide a radiant picture. Don't forget to look away from a setting sun and note its effect on your subject.

Kodachrome 64, 1/125 sec, f8

LOWER RIGHT: Ribbons of steel, a painted sky, and a train growling toward the distant horizon share in composing a mood on film. Here the red marker on the caboose punctuates the scene and the color of the sky is reflected in the rails.

Kodachrome 64, 1/125 sec, f5.6

FOLLOWING PAGE TOP LEFT: Sunsets develop, change quickly, and disappear very fast. Don't wait for what you feel may be the best picture. Continue to take photos as the colors change. In this photo, a superb western sky furnished the stage for a solid, bold three-quarter diesel shot.

Ektachrome 64, 1/125 sec, f5.6

FOLLOWING PAGE LOWER LEFT: Both the setting sun and the standing water contribute to the composition of this photo. Strong silhouettes are duplicated by the mirror effect of the water. Always "looking for a photo" is the essence of photography.

Kodachrome 64, 1/60 sec, f5.6

FOLLOWING PAGE RIGHT: Pollution, one of our modern contributions, helps create the red or orange sun disk. In this "look-down" shot, an empty grain train rolls in from the west. The warm tones impart a rich color spectrum when photographed in the light of a setting sun.

Ektachrome 100, 1/250 sec, f5.6

All Photos Roger M. Ingbretsen

PRECEDING PAGE: A sunset can add to the natural lure of faraway places, travel, and railroads. Because sunsets have such a universal appeal, even a cold winter setting can spark interest in your photo.

Ektachrome 1/125 sec, f5.6

Roger M. Ingbretsen

FACING PAGE: Bold lines, sharply defined silhouettes, and a tinge of color are all elements available during the low light conditions of sunset. The electrical tower of a turntable serves as a frame for this diesel engine as it stands idle in an engine service facility. Note how the oil spills in the foreground are highlighted when photographed in reflective low light conditions.

Ektachrome 64, 1/125 sec, f5.6

Roger M. Ingbretsen

ABOVE: Exploit different shooting angles and take full advantage of the lighting conditions available during sunsets. Remember also to use a tripod during low light photography as the lens will be almost wide open and movement will ruin your photographic efforts.

Roger M. Ingbretsen

ABOVE: The pine tree at the left blocked any direct sunlight into the camera lens. The results were a silhouette of the tree, excellent sidelighting of a speeding train, and great definition of the snow-covered ground detail. This was a planned shot and required several trips back to the same location. Waiting for a train to appear at the right time and under the right conditions can pay off. Ektachrome 64, 1/250 sec, f5.6

RIGHT: 'Ribbons of steel" and the classic "ride off into the sunset" scene remain a proven success formula in railroad photography. Kodachrome 64, 1/125 sec, f5.6

All Photos by Roger M. Ingbretsen

7

The Warmth of
EARLY
MORNING
and
LATE
AFTERNOON

These are the restful periods of the day. As the warmth of a new day starts and as the heat of day begins to melt into evening, the time to photograph action on the rails is ideal. The quality of light, not quantity, is the positive factor.

Three words take on special meaning during these times of day: shadow, form, and texture.

SHADOW:

The harshness of high sunlight is diffused and broken into shafts of light or sidelight, striking objects at lower angles. Shadows, which begin to form, highlight the subject or create additional patterns, interest, and variety. Strong shadows can emphasize the brightness of contrasting colors. Exaggerated shadows can minimize or tone down unwanted foreground detail. Shadows can also be very important in shaping a subject. They provide that extra ingredient needed for depth, contour, and form.

Light, as always, is an important factor. Together, the interaction of light and shadow create that strong sense of form for impact. Again, impact is what a creative photo is all about.

FORM:

Form is a side effect of contrast. Stated another way, low sunlight adds the right amount of contrast. As you wait for the time of day to change, you can control the natural light and contrast within the picture.

The effects of sidelighting and low natural lighting combine to create "depth" in your railroad photos. Form adds both depth and volume to the width and height of your subject. As bold and big as most railroad subjects are, low light photography can contribute to an even greater degree and help define more dramatically the form of a massive engine.

TEXTURE:

To show texture, light must slant across a surface. Low or oblique lighting enhances the texture of virtually any surface, whereas the high noonday sunlight eliminates the rich benefit of texture. In high sun, a box car can appear to be just that, a metal box. During the low-level natural lighting conditions prevalent during early or late hours, that same metal box can take on strong characteristics. Rivet and brace detail show up distinctly, giving definite structural strength to the subject. Additionally, this detail provides the patterns necessary to aid in the creation of an impact photo.

The warm, golden glow from an early morning or late afternoon sun will help you create that distinctive mood present in creative photography. Your goal is to exploit the use of natural lighting extremes. As in almost all low light conditions, infinite, creative variety is the reward when developing low light photographic techniques. When mixed with the photographer's paintbrush — "light" — , shadow, form, and texture are the key ingredients.

PRECEDING PAGE LARGE: A placid, warm scene can be shot during the early morning or the late afternoon when water tends to be calmer and the sun's tones tend to be soft. Notice how the colors in the mirror-like surface of the river are deeper than the actual subject. The mood of the photograph is contrary to the actual setting. The photo was taken from a highway bridge with rush-hour traffic at the photographer's back.
Ektachrome 64
Robert L. Hundman

PRECEDING PAGE SMALL: A very shallow sun angle created this spectacular lighting of SP 4449 and its train at Oceana, California.
Fuji Film
Jay Williams

RIGHT: When you set your sights on a location that is going to be good for sunset or sunrise, keep your eyes open for opportunities that will present themselves should a train arrive early or late. Here with the sun too high to give dramatic colors, drama is still achieved by hiding the sun behind the signal mast and gaining the reflections off the side of the oncoming train.
Roger M. Ingbretsen

FOLLOWING PAGE TOP: Jay Williams caught "The Coast Daylight-Starlight" at San Lucas in March of 1986. Notice how the variation in lighting between this photo and the photo on page 85 change the mood.　　　Fuji Film
Jay Williams

FOLLOWING PAGE BOTTOM: The dry, yellow grass in the foreground picks up the sunlight and produces excellent front-to-back interest in this photo. One hazard to watch for is the shadow of yourself or other objects when the sun is behind you.
Kodachrome 64, 1/125 sec, f5.6
Tim Lund

FACING PAGE: The tonal range in this picture goes from black to muted tan on the main subject. The golden sunlight coming from the left provides excellent definition on the engine side. This is contrasted by lack of detail on the darkened front. Ektachrome, 1/125 sec, f5.6
Robert L. Hundman

A different "going-away-from-the-photographer" picture is just another example of how you can vary composition. The undercarriage of the equipment becomes a point of interest as it is exposed by the extreme low sunlight.

Ektachrome 64, 1/250 sec, f5.6

Walter Olevsky

FACING PAGE: The low sun in early morning hours gives a clarity not achieved at any other time of day. Here, the newly painted Washington Central equipment is bathed in that early light and the colors are exceptionally strong. Watch for this kind of situation.
Rick Leach

TOP: The low light in this mountain scene has emphasized the red marker light that punctuates the tail end of this stainless steel "hotel-on-wheels." Don't put your camera away when the light begins to fade!
Kodachrome 64, 1/250 sec, f5.6
Reed McNaught

ABOVE: Note how the exhaust is given more highlight by the low light of evening. The glass-like pond lends an air of tranquility as the passenger train glides by. Kodachrome 64, 1/250 sec, f5.6
Reed McNaught

ABOVE: Early morning sunlight aids in defining shapes.
In this photo, it also provides extreme contrast to put the subject in
a dramatic spotlight.   Ektachrome

Robert L. Hundman

RIGHT: A classic "look-down" low light shot combines bold color,
sharp contrast, and the nostalgic beauty of a steam locomotive
racing for the next stop.   Ektachrome 64, 1/250 sec, f11

Jay Williams

FOLLOWING PAGE: Here is a photo that combines both an
overcast day, a bit of mist falling, and so late in the day that the
light would normally be expected to give you a picture of no value
at all. However, by carefully positioning the dwarf signal and
getting the headlights on the train as well, an interesting shot is
achieved. If you'll watch for this kind of situation, you can produce
photographs of both drama and mood.   Roger M. Ingbretsen

FOLLOWING PAGE INSETS – LEFT: Peeking through the clouds,
the sun paints a beautiful silver sky while the dark outline of a local
freight rambles slowly across the bridge. The weeds in the lower
left balance the main subject which is almost totally in the right half
of the picture.   Roger M. Ingbretsen
CENTER: The dark outline of the diesels roll slowly onto the bridge.
Note how the weeds and low brush in the foreground and the
distant mountains give depth to the overall scene.   Tim Lund
RIGHT: A strong silhouette shot of the train and bridge is made
possible by putting the low sun directly behind the center abutment
of the bridge. Learning to use the sun in as many different settings
as possible and shooting from as many angles as possible can add
variety to your photographic endeavors. Kodachrone 64, 1/125 sec
Roger M. Ingbretsen

8

The Magic of
NIGHT

Although railroads are an around-the-clock business, railfan photographers rarely capture the magic of the industry under the dark blanket of night. For reasons still not clear to me, taking pictures at night was the last hurdle I overcame in my creative photographic endeavor. Early one morning, while on a sunrise photo excursion, I turned to the west and noticed the moon's shining surface just above an engine standing at the sand servicing tower. Snapping a few pictures was what I consider my start of night photography — that is, from twilight to just before sunrise.

The best time to catch the effects of moonlight is when a full moon is coming up over the horizon. Just before the sun rises in the east is also a great time to catch the full moon in a low western sky. The advantage of these two times is that the moon itself reflects little light on your rail scene. The small extra light that remains in the sky at dusk and dawn add just enough to allow a short exposure time. This low light condition will, in some instances, even permit hand-held shots with fast film. They'll also pick up detail not available in total darkness. With the right lens opening, many rail scenes taken at dusk or dawn can actually give more realistic results than what may be called genuine night photographs.

If weather conditions are basically clear, you'll have seven days per month to photograph a full moon: three days before, during, and three days after. For a few days after a full moon, the moon will still appear full and visible in the western sky just as the sun is starting to light a new day.

Bracketing your exposures will allow you to pick the picture providing the best "moon mood." One word of caution on moon photography. Exposures of more than one second will cause a blurring of the moon to occur due to its fast movement relative to the earth.

Light sources other than the moon are also available at night. Large banks of floodlights are usually located in rail yards. The lights on freight or passenger stations and engine servicing facilities can also be used as a light source and for contrast. Add rain to these railroad night scenes, and the reflection from standing water will increase visible detail and create vivid patterns. Snow also has excellent reflective properties at night. The snow will enhance the color of both natural and artificial light. A simple emergency source of light for your favorite railroad subject is your car. Turn your high beams on and light up or flood the area you wish to photograph.

The use of a tripod for other than dusk, dawn, or brightly lit subjects is a must. For speeds slower than one second, the use of a cable release is suggested to prevent jarring the camera. Exposure settings for night photography are very hard to predict; however, the following provides you with a general guide. As pointed out several times in this book, don't fail to bracket your photos one or two stops in either direction. Also, for night pictures, experiment with longer and shorter time exposures for the best results.

Subject	ASA 64	ASA 400
Brightly lighted station	1/2 sec. at f2	1/2 sec. at f4
Rail yard scene just after sunset	2 sec. at f2.8	1 sec. at f5.6
Floodlighted yard	1 sec. at f2.8	1/2 sec. at f5.6
Rail scene lighted by full moon	4 min. at f4*	30 sec. at f2.8*

*Cut time in half if photographed in snow.

If your camera has a "B" setting on the shutter speed dial, a cable release can be used in conjunction with this feature for long exposures. After you depress the plunger of the cable release, lock it. The shutter will stay open until you unlock the plunger. This is a great configuration if you want to "fire flash." You can set the f-stop at 5.6, lock the plunger, use an electronic flash attachment, and flash different parts of a locomotive. (Note: Be sure to release the plunger after approximately three to five minutes.) This technique will highlight and fill in dark, shadowy areas for a nice effect. Your image will not be picked up on film as long as you keep moving.

If your camera has an auto-focusing feature (many non-SLR 35mm cameras do), try using it for photographing your night scenes. You'll have to use a tripod, because your lens will stay open for periods of time exceeding hand-held operation. This auto-focusing feature takes much of the guess-work out of night exposure scenes. It also adds a basic technique which can produce good results.

There is a variety of possibilities when you consider the many light sources available at night and the capabilities of your camera. The special ability of film, which can add up light and reproduce colors we cannot see with the human eye at night, is definitely worth pursuing.

PRECEDING PAGE LARGE: With the camera set on "B" for three minutes at f5.6, the magic of night at a busy engine facility is captured on film. There are other lights on an engine besides a head-light. This is very evident in this photo which shows lighted number boards, running lights, anti-collision lights, step lights, and service lights over the tracks. Note also each type of light looks different in color when developed on film.
Ektachrome film
Roger M. Ingbretsen

PRECEDING PAGE SMALL: Here the lighted sand tower is the center attraction with the engine standing in the shadows. A secondary focal point is the moon shining through an overcast sky. Exposures of more than one minute will cause a blurring of the moon to occur due to its fast movement relative to the earth.
Ektachrome, 1 min, f5.6
Roger M. Ingbretsen

RIGHT: The dwarf signal at Trowbridge Junction in East Lansing, Michigan shows how an otherwise bland picture can become special when taken at night.
Kodachrome
Ron Hagemeister

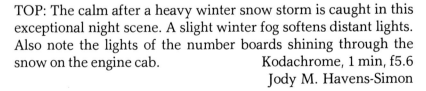

TOP: The calm after a heavy winter snow storm is caught in this exceptional night scene. A slight winter fog softens distant lights. Also note the lights of the number boards shining through the snow on the engine cab.   Kodachrome, 1 min, f5.6
Jody M. Havens-Simon

ABOVE: Rail action does not stop when the sun goes down. Many interesting photographs can be shot with the aid of a tripod and longer exposures. Note the crisp icy feeling created in this scene. Also, the movement of the train at the extreme right gives action to this night shot.   Kodachrome
Ronald Hagemeister

ABOVE: From the star burst headlight at the front to the stainless steel fluted sides of the passenger cars, this night scene conjures up the romantic nostalgia of passenger train travel.

Ektachrome, 2 min, f5.6

Roger M. Ingbretsen

TOP LEFT: The famous "F units" of the Rio Grande are pictured in this superb night photo. The glow of the city lights imparts a blue-green haze to the night sky. Many different sources of light truly make this an interesting night photograph.   B. Nall

TOP RIGHT: An Amtrak locomotive with a spectacular city background just begs for a time exposure.   Kodochrome, Roger M. Ingbretsen

ABOVE LEFT: Late night travelers can relate to this special "mood" photograph. The snow and ice all around make the warmth of the station even more inviting.   Greg Konnrad

ABOVE RIGHT: A long four minute exposure imparts strong definition to the beams of light coming from the duel headlights of this standing engine.   Fred M. Simon

FACING PAGE: The yellow color of this "Chessie" diesel stands out well in the night sky. The "sleeping cat" insignia on the nose of the engine is symbolic of the night but not of the action which can be shot during the dark hours. Observe the detail of the cab interior. This cannot be seen in a daylight photo.   Kodachrome film
Ronald Hagemeister

Escaping steam on a cold night
provides an air of interest in this picture.
Steam was most always a key ingredient
when photographing steam locomotives
of the past but it can still be found with
today's diesels. Look for it and
use it when you can.
Kodachrome, 10 sec, f5.6
Jay Williams

9

The Art of
COMPOSING
Railfan Pictures

Like any type or form of photography, creative railfan pictures need something significant to catch the viewer's eye — some detail or object to draw the eye to a particular part or parts of the scene. This technique is what separates a mere snapshot from a composed, creative piece of photography. Rather than just simply taking pictures, it's important for a photographer to think about what is going to be done or what mood is to be portrayed. A massive diesel engine can be the center of interest in a picture; however, where the engine is placed in the picture, the angle used, the background, foreground, lighting, and placement of surrounding equipment or people all go into "making" a picture. What may seem like a dramatic railroad scene to you (by virtue of actually being there) may come through in a photo as just a so-so picture.

A camera sees in only two dimensions. You must create depth, because a lens does not see in the three dimensions we do. Several techniques can be used, however, to create this "third dimension."

To give extra depth to a picture, locate something in the foreground. An example might be a switch stand, a pile of railroad ties, a sign, or a signal light. This creates a feeling of depth and draws subtle attention to your subject. Side or backlighting can also create a feeling of distance. High noon sun shots or front-lighting provide the truest colors, but they also give the flattest most non-dimensional, blah picture.

Most people simply stand in front of, or to the side of, an oncoming train and snap a picture. To heighten interest, try to find a high or low vantage point. A low angle shot looking up at an engine can create a more impressive and powerful look. A low angle shot can also be used to eliminate clutter from the surrounding area, placing the outline of your rail equipment against the sky.

A high angle "look-down" shot can reveal many details not usually seen by a railfan. Cooling fans, blackened exhaust stacks, and the weathered tops of rolling stock are just a sample of the photographic possibilities. So, before you shoot, walk around using your view finder to compose and to decide which angle will give you the most interesting, expressive picture.

Shadows are also an important element of rail photography, because they define form. Sidelighting at approximately 45 degrees or less can heighten detail on the surface of rail equipment to create texture. This is because the small shadows exaggerate and emphasize any slight changes in a surface. A shaft of light penetrating the subdued shadows of an engine house can create a feeling of the musty grit usually associated with such a place. Strong shadows on the front of an oncoming engine can emphasize the brightness of a headlight — even during daylight hours.

Don't get hung up on the "rules" of photography. Break the rules, and you'll be surprised at the results. Shoot into the sun, take pictures in low light, bad weather, and at angles not normally attempted by most photographers. Try seeing things from a different perspective and then use your camera to create that image. Like an artist in other mediums, you can develop a style and convey to others the world of railroading from your unique viewpoint.

PRECEDING PAGE LARGE: Although this scene has a tremendous amount of clutter, the bright, red engine overrides the confusion and establishes a center point of interest. Watch for spots of color in an otherwise monochromatic scene.
Ektachrome 64, 1/250 sec, f8
Roger M. Ingbretsen

PRECEDING PAGE SMALL: Severe contrast between the dark shadows at the left and the bright, yellow cab at the right adds a distinctive boldness to this "look-down" shot.
Ektachrome 100, 1/500 sec, f11
Roger M. Ingbretsen

RIGHT: The simplest of subjects can provide a dramatic photo if the lighting is right. Here a pair of searchlight signals is silhouetted against a slightly colored sky at sunset.
Kodachrome
Bob Zenk

PAGE 112: A mountain stream in the Canadian Rockies and the plush green of early summer wrap this bright red Canadian Pacific diesel in natural beauty.
Ektachrome 100, 1/250 sec, f11
Roger M. Ingbretsen

PAGE 113 TOP: The main subject doesn't always need to be close to the camera. Putting distance between you and the subject, but filling in with interesting foreground, can help to compose a picture with feeling.
Ektachrome 100
Roger M. Ingbretsen

PAGE 113 BOTTOM: In still another mountain stream scene, the bright red engines are the center attraction; however, the stream, forests, and sky all catch the eye of the viewer. The placement of the railroad equipment in the right surroundings goes a long way toward making that creative railroad picture.
Ektachrome 100, 1/250 sec, f8
Roger M. Ingbretsen

TOP LEFT: A great amount of depth is created in this photo. Note how the downward slope of the first three mountains and the high peak of the farthest range all converge or surround the center of our subject — the train.

Kodachrome 64, 1/125 sec, f8

Fred Simon

TOP RIGHT: Contrast is one of the many basic tools used when composing a picture. Here the bright, yellow Union Pacific passenger train stands out strikingly well against a darkened gray, stormy sky. The sun coming in from the left has also highlighted the silver trucks of the engine and cars.

Kodachrome 64, 1/125 sec, f8

Bledsoe Rail Slides

ABOVE LEFT: Sunlight pouring through a window and the Black background can intensify colors. Such is the case with this photo.

Fuji Film

Jay Williams

ABOVE RIGHT: The Southern Pacific photo at Langtry, Texas provides an example of making the best of unusual lighting. The sun is almost in line with the train, but slightly to the other side, giving a silhouetted effect. The low sun angle dramatizes the scenery.

Kodachrome

Reed McNaught

FACING PAGE: High sunlight can definitely highlight the subject. A clear, blue sky and the red, white, and blue stripes on the Amtrak engines stand out against the green trees and various shades of rock.

Walter Olevsky

RAILROAD CROSSING

10

The
OTHER
WORLD
In Railroading

As in many occupations, the outsider looks at railroading with fascination and a naive sense of romanticism. But what about the individuals who have worked a lifetime in the tough world of steam, ash, diesel oil, and steel? What do they see? What kind of equipment occupies the long and, in some cases, weather-beaten hours of their day? Well, it's no doubt hard for a non-railroader/photographer to slip into the heavy overalls of a trainman, or the leather gloves of a gandy dancer, but it's worth a try.

The thrust of this final section is to show the many "other" photographic aspects of railroads. We'll look at the signals an engineer sees and at the view from a conductor's standpoint. We'll take a creative look at what there is to photograph besides a three-quarter shot of a locomotive. We'll take a pictorial glimpse at the nuts and bolts of the industry we call railroading.

Let's start with the four basics: wooden ties, tie plates, spikes, and rails. These components are the foundation of our entire rail system. Much of the trackwork is older than the equipment rolling on it; however, it is through the constant care and repair that these small, but most important, parts of the system remain serviceable. Reportedly, one-fifth to one-fourth of most railroads' revenue is directed toward the maintenance of rail and roadbed. Trackwork photographed in the right light, right angle, or creative setting can vividly portray the feeling of travel, adventure, or the sheer power and size of railroads. Even as separate components, interesting patterns with fascinating texture can be caught by the lens. A pile of spikes, a stack of ties, or a bed of rails can offer the chance to experiment.

Signals and signs serve as the guideposts for keeping the entire rail system moving smoothly. Other chapters have referred to their use in helping create a balance; however, signals and signs by themselves can serve as very interesting subjects. Backlighting by the sun, early morning, late evening, or low light conditions can have a dramatic effect on a normal "run-of-the-mill" sign or signal. I first discovered this while waiting for a train that never arrived. The sun was well above the hori-zon. In a state of frustration, I snapped a picture of a silhouetted semaphore signal. The results were rewarding and opened up a new photographic avenue to pursue when train traffic was slow.

Switch towers, water towers, sand towers, bridges, tunnels, snowplows, maintenance shacks, and end bumpers are just a sampling of what the railroad has to offer as photographic subjects. The purpose of your photography is to be creative, so look for the unusual and the interesting. Think and feel your subject. Picture what you're going after. And . . . always be open to and look for a new picture to portray the excitement, charm, and nostalgia of railroading.

PRECEDING PAGE LARGE: There are many railfans who would classify a city light rail rapid transit system as a railroad; however, most railroad photographers don't take advantage of these colorful units. A late afternoon sun and a threatening gray sky actually heighten the crimson red of the main subject in this picture.
Ektachrome 64, 1/250 sec, f11
Walter Olevsky

PRECEDING PAGE SMALL: The gray, weathered cross arms are a familiar sight to virtually everyone. It's a simple, but interesting subject.
Ektachrome 64, 1/250 sec, f11
Robert L. Hundman

TOP RIGHT: Artificial lighting and the intracacy of truss bridge latticework provide a subject with tremendous possibilities. It's also one you don't have to wait for.
Roger M. Ingbretsen

BOTTOM RIGHT: Interior and exterior lighting of this Amtrak Superliner provide an interesting study in color variations.
Fred M. Simon

PAGE 126 TOP: Patiently waiting for the right conditions resulted in the shooting of this track grinding machine. The late afternoon and a gray day helped emphasize the sparks generated by the grinding wheels on the rails. If this same photo had been shot on a bright sunny day, the action would not have been as exciting and colorful.
Kodachrome 64, 1/125 sec, f5.6
Roger M. Ingbretsen

PAGE 126 BOTTOM: The maintenance of the right-of-way is a never ending and tough job. Here the action of steel being welded is captured as "the pot" melts down, binding the ribbons of steel.
Kodachrome 64, 1/250 sec, f11
Roger M. Ingbretsen

PAGE 127: Use a little inventiveness for rainy day photos. Here, stepping into the engine house provides natural framing for a photo that might otherwise be bland.
Ektachrome
Robert L. Hundman

PAGE 128 TOP: The same location, but a different time, illustrate how the sun can be used in various ways to showcase your subject. The sun cresting an eastern horizon imparts warmth to this photo of whistle sign and rail.
Kodachrome 64, 1/125 sec, f5.6
Roger M. Ingbretsen

PAGE 128 BOTTOM: Shooting directly into the sun and using the same whistle sign as a shield was the technique used in the lower photograph. This was a "planned" shot after discovering the cutout "W" type of sign.
Kodachrome 64, 1/250 sec, f16
Roger M. Ingbretsen

PAGE 129: Converging rails are always an excellent subject and, although every picture in this book was taken with a standard lens, a telephoto lens can draw those distant signals in even closer.
Ektachrome
Roger M. Ingbretsen

ABOVE: The "dispatcher's desk" is a difficult scene to find because of its disappearance from the modern railroad scene. Many railroad men can relate to the long hours spent waiting for the next train to call in. Had this photo been taken at night, the mood would have been "truer."

Ektachrome 64, 1/125 sec, f8
Walter Olevsky

FACING PAGE: The heavy, wooden timbers of a tunnel lining and the silver rails spiked down to the creosote cross ties spell railroad. Except for those railroad crews who ride the rails, this scene is not viewed by many. This may be an acceptable shot from the other end of the tunnel, but don't place yourself in a precarious situation.

Ektachrome 100, 1 sec, f32
Roger M. Ingbretsen

TOP LEFT: When shown to a retired railroad conductor, this photo spurred a long discussion about the countless, beautiful sunrises and sunsets he had witnessed over his forty years of riding the rails. When something like this happens, you know you've "captured" feeling in your photography.
Kodachrome 64, 1/125 sec, f5.6
Roger M. Ingbretsen

TOP RIGHT: The sun backlights a semaphore signal. This type of signal is disappearing quickly, so don't overlook them as photographic material.
Kodachrome 64, 1/250 sec, f11
Tim Lund

ABOVE LEFT: Given the right conditions, a switch stand and the associated trackwork can provide a striking picture. Interesting patterns, fascinating texture, and a splash of color have all been caught in this creative photo.
Kodachrome 64, 1/60 sec, f11
Bill Taylor

ABOVE RIGHT: A pattern of circles is formed by these rust-coated wheel sets. The subjects are there. All you have to do is 'look and see" a picture possibility.
Kodachrome 64, 1/125 sec, f8
Roger M. Ingbretsen

The cross arms of a rail crossing sign provide a very "railroady" feeling in this picture. It is a scene which almost any motorist can relate to. Taking an everday situation and recording it on film under the right conditions is worth the effort. Ektachrome 64, 1/250 sec, f5.6

Roger M. Ingbretsen

LEFT: A "part of the whole" is an interesting approach. Getting in close and photographing only a part of this steam engine from a low angle has provided an overpowering perspective of the massive drive wheels. Walk around the subject, look through the view finder from all angles, and create a picture.

Ektachrome 64, 1/60 sec, f16
Walter Olevsky

ABOVE: These freshly painted silver signals and the accompanying equipment box stand out exceptionally against the dark sky. The side low light of the sun overemphasizes the subject.

Kodachrome 64, 1/125 sec, f5.6
Fred M. Simon